DAVID BROWN
TRACTORS

Jonathan Whitlam

AMBERLEY

First published 2017

Amberley Publishing
The Hill, Stroud,
Gloucestershire, GL5 4EP

www.amberley-books.com

ISBN: 978 1 4456 6554 2 (print)
ISBN: 978 1 4456 6555 9 (ebook)

British Library Cataloguing in Publication Data.
A catalogue record for this book is available from the British Library.

Typeset in 10pt on 13pt Celeste.
Typesetting by Amberley Publishing.
Printed in the UK.

Contents

Introduction

The firm of David Brown was established in the Yorkshire town of Huddersfield in 1860, with gear wheel manufacture soon becoming its main source of business. David Brown, who had a grandson of the same name, started the firm, and it was this second David Brown that got the firm into the tractor-building business.

The first signs of an interest in tractors saw the David Brown company supplying gear components to Irish engineer Harry Ferguson to use in a prototype tractor he was building, which became known as the Black Tractor thanks to its all-over colour. When Ferguson failed to interest any firms in putting his prototype into production, he turned to David Brown to manufacture the tractor for him to sell as the Ferguson Type A.

Harry Ferguson and his small team of engineers had been working on a system of making implements part of the tractor itself and with the Ferguson Type A they managed to revolutionise mechanised farming forever. The Ferguson System consisted of a form of hydraulic draft control teamed with a three-point linkage, which connected with specially made implements to form an integral unit and allowed this relatively small tractor to pull well beyond its weight. The Ferguson System also made the tractor safer, as the weight transfer it gave from the implement to the front of the tractor stopped the machine rearing up backwards if the implement hit a solid obstruction in the soil.

The first Ferguson tractors, built at the David Brown Park Works in Huddersfield, and painted in all-over grey at Ferguson's insistence, used a 20 hp Coventry Climax Type E engine, which could be constructed to run on either straight petrol or on paraffin. From 1937, a David Brown-manufactured engine replaced the Climax unit, using the same casting machinery that was bought from Climax by David Brown. Drive was taken through a three forward and single reverse gearbox and the tractor was constructed very much along the lines of the already very successful Fordson tractor, although the Ferguson System made all the difference to performance, provided the correct implements were used.

It took until 1938 before rear mudguards were fitted; previous to this there was no such luxury item and even then it was still an optional extra. A rare orchard version, which was lower and much narrower, was also offered, but did not sell in large numbers.

Around 1,350 Ferguson Type A tractors had been built by the time this restored example came along. Painted in all-over grey, the Type A conformed to Harry Ferguson's ideal in that everything was functional with no unnecessary trimmings.

The revolutionary end of the Ferguson Type A was the three-point linkage at the rear, but this was also a problem in that to get the best out of this little tractor the farmer also needed to buy an assortment of specially built implements.

Although the Ferguson name was carried prominently on the top of the front radiator, David Brown Tractors Ltd, the company set up by Mr David Brown to build the machines, affixed a small metal plate to the bottom of the radiator, hence many enthusiasts calling the Type A the 'Ferguson-Brown'.

The little Ferguson tractor worked very well but there was a problem; a prospective purchaser not only had to buy the tractor, which cost twice as much as a Fordson Model N, but also the special implements, making it even more expensive. The result was that unsold tractors started to build up. David Brown suggested several changes to the design to make it more sellable but Harry Ferguson was having none of it and went to the USA to meet with Henry Ford; the Ford 9N with the Ferguson System duly appeared in 1939.

David Brown was not content with leaving the tractor industry and, despite still having stocks of the Ferguson Type A to sell, designed his own tractor, which would also see the light of day in 1939. Harry Ferguson would go on to produce his own tractors again in 1946, and do it very successfully, but the Irish inventor had started David Brown on a new path – one that would see it go from producing gears to tractors. This book is the story of the machines it built.

CHAPTER 1

Hunting Pink is the Colour

When David Brown launched the VAK1 at the Royal Show at Windsor in 1939, it certainly looked different to the Ferguson Type A, or the Ferguson-Brown as it was often called.

First off was the colour; gone was the drab all-over grey that Ferguson had insisted on, and instead the new tractor looked resplendent in a new 'Hunting Pink' livery, which certainly made it stand out. It was also of a completely different design to anything that had been seen before, including a large cast-iron grille hiding the radiator that was replaced on later tractors with sheet steel, and soon became dubbed the 'bullet hole' grille due to its round holes. A type of windshield was also fitted around the front of the driver's platform, which later gained the title of a 'scuttle', and the bonnet was more streamlined than the Ferguson Type A.

The model name VAK1 was actually an acronym, standing for Vehicle Agricultural Kerosene 1. Power came from an overhead valve, four-cylinder David Brown engine that produced 35 hp, and a four forward and single reverse gearbox was fitted. Power take-off was an option but hydraulics were not initially, a new design using a depth wheel to control implement height being offered from 1941, which was not as sophisticated as that fitted to the Ferguson Type A so that no patents were infringed. The VAK1 was available with either a petrol or paraffin-fuelled engine and was built in a newly acquired factory that used to be a mill, hence its name of Meltham Mills. Situated about five miles from Huddersfield, Mr David Brown acquired the site after his father refused him more space in Park Works for tractor building. From now on Meltham Mills would be the centre for all David Brown tractor manufacturing and would build tractors right up to 1988.

The VTK crawler was really a tracked version of the VAK1, the letters this time standing for Vehicle Tracked Kerosene. Designed for use on the grass runways cropping up in Britain following the outbreak of the Second World War, the VTK was primarily used as an aircraft tug but proved to be too slow, leading to the development of the VIG 1/100 – the Vehicle Industrial Gasoline 1, which was back on wheels but equipped with a heavy sub-frame into which weights could be placed as ballast. A big winch was fitted to the rear, built by David Brown themselves, and the tractor had a very impressive pulling ability. Many of these industrial machines were actually converted VTK crawlers. When the war finished some of these machines had a front pulley fitted, enabling them to be used to power threshing drums, hence the new name used for them – Thresherman.

This brilliantly restored David Brown VAK1 clearly shows what the tractor would have looked like when new, right down to the steel wheels. It looked very different to the Ferguson Type A and the new 'Hunting Pink' colour certainly made it stand out.

This later VAK1 has a different front radiator grille treatment but the lines of the bonnet are the same, including the 'scuttle' around the front of the driving platform.

A 35 hp David Brown four-cylinder engine resided under the streamlined bonnet of the VAK1. Note the air pre-cleaner that rises up beside the engine.

The Thresherman was born out of the conversion of wartime VTK crawlers. As can be seen, the fitting of long mudguards and a front pulley positioned in front of the bonnet made a very workmanlike machine.

David Brown had not finished with crawler manufacture however, and although the first attempt had been something of a failure, the next venture, the DB4, certainly was not. Built under license from the Caterpillar company in the USA, the DB4 was very similar to the Caterpillar D4 but used a Dorman diesel engine of 38.5 hp, making it the very first David Brown machine to be fitted with a diesel power unit. Clutch and brake steering was used and drive was taken through a five-speed gearbox and a great number of them would be used by the British Army during the war, with production not finishing until 1949.

The VAK1A replaced the original model in 1945 and shared the same basic styling but had a longer wheelbase and modified front axles as well as an improved engine with a quicker warm-up period. Looking very similar to the first model, the most obvious external differences were probably the use of a square-type front axle and the pressed steel grille with horizontal bars concealing the radiator at the front.

In 1947, the first really successful David Brown tractor made its appearance in the shape of the similar looking VAK1C, otherwise known to one and all as the Cropmaster. The fact that the new model was given a name helped to publicise it at a time when there was a great hunger for tractors on British farms after the war and when growing food was still a national concern. A four forward and single reverse transmission was still fitted, but from 1949 it made history when it was updated with a six-speed transmission and a two-speed power take-off: the first British-built tractor to be so equipped. It was also in 1949 that a diesel engine was offered for the first time, with a power rating of 34 hp, and built by David Brown in-house, making the company the first to build their own multi-cylinder diesel tractor engine. David Brown also produced variants of the base model with narrow vineyard and industrial machines, including the Taskmaster.

The second type of David Brown crawler was much more successful than the first. The DB4 was actually built under license from Caterpillar as much of its design was based on the American D4 crawler. David Brown chose a Dorman diesel engine as a power source and the British Army made good use of them during the Second World War.

The driving platform of the DB4, showing the very minimal dashboard of the era with very few dials and gauges.

Arriving in 1945, the VAK1A replaced the original model and featured a modified front axle arrangement as well as quicker engine starting.

The VAK1C appeared in 1947 but was known much more commonly as the David Brown Cropmaster.

The design of the Cropmaster was very closely based on the earlier tractors but was neatened up in small areas and now featured the David Brown name vertically down the centre of the radiator grille.

This was the view that greeted the driver of the Cropmaster: a neatly laid out dashboard with limited equipment, steering wheel and column mounted to the right-hand side and, of course, the famous 'scuttle' around the front.

A David Brown Cropmaster working with a binder at a show in the south of England. [Photo: Kim Parks]

In 1950 the Super Cropmaster arrived with a 38 hp TVO engine and a faster speed than the standard Cropmaster. A similar Prairie Cropmaster was also built from 1951, but without the by now trademark double seat, and was sold mainly into the North American market, hence its name.

The Trackmaster 30, based on the ubiquitous Cropmaster, replaced the DB4 in 1950. A larger version appeared in 1952 in the shape of the Trackmaster Diesel 50, which used a six-cylinder engine.

It was all change in 1953 when a whole new range of tractors replaced the earlier models and used a new numbering system to tell the various models apart. Externally the new tractors looked very much like the Cropmaster, although in fact they were, if anything, stripped-down versions, with much less metal used in their construction and the much-loved scuttle and bench seat deleted, except for on some very early models.

The smallest was the 25, which used a 31 hp petrol or 32 hp vaporising oil engine, followed by the 25D, the diesel engine of which was rated at 31 hp. The 30C had a 37.5 hp petrol or 34 hp TVO engine while the 30D was once again the diesel version, this time with 41 hp available. A six-speed transmission was fitted to all these models and there were also two reverse gears, while an improved hydraulic system saw the advent of the David Brown TCU in 1954, which stood for Traction Control Unit, and which still needed the implement being used to be fitted with a depth wheel to get around the Ferguson patents. TCU worked well though, as it transferred more weight onto the tractor to limit wheelslip. In 1955 this was supplemented by the availability of a special hitch that could be used to transfer weight from four-wheeled trailers and trailed implements.

The Super Cropmaster joined the standard model in 1950 with 38 hp and a faster speed.

Fluted side panels encased the engine on the Super Cropmaster, as shown on this example at a rally in Suffolk.

Although not physically larger than the standard version, the Super Cropmaster somehow looked more imposing. The David Brown four-cylinder engine ran on Tractor Vaporising Oil.

The Cropmaster tractors disappeared in 1953 in favour of a range of three models available with differently fuelled engines. Smallest was the 25C with either petrol or TVO fuelling, giving either 31 hp or 32 hp respectively.

The 25D was the diesel variant, once again a David Brown unit and with a 31 hp rating.

This 25D is shown at a show with a David Brown Albion baler in tow.

The 30D was a bigger tractor powered by a 41 hp diesel engine, making this quite a powerful machine for its size.

A close-up of the bonnet of the 30D shows how similar it was to the earlier tractors. In many ways these machines were stripped-down versions of the Cropmaster, with fewer standard features to keep costs down.

This preserved 30D looks stunning on the rally field and shows that it was quite a long tractor when seen in profile.

This high-clearance 30D was produced for use with Chafer sprayers.

A new, bigger tractor was also unveiled. The 50D was basically a wheeled version of the largest crawler, with 50 hp available from a six-cylinder diesel engine. This was a seriously big tractor back then and took David Brown into the large power bracket for the first time. British farmers were not yet ready to accept this level of power output though and the great majority of the 50D tractors produced were exported overseas.

Crawlers were still in the mix with the earlier two smaller models rebadged as the 30T and 30TD, while the big Trackmaster 50 Diesel became the 50TD. David Brown had been making a range of implements to go with its tractors from the beginning, learning from the original plans of Harry Ferguson. In 1955 this was taken a step further when Harrison, McGregor & Guest, based at Leigh in Lancashire, was taken over by David Brown, which then resulted in many more pieces of farm machinery joining the line-up, including forage harvesters, balers and even a trailed combine.

It was also in 1955 that David Brown launched a very unusual little tractor. The 2D was a 14 hp tool-carrier with a rear-mounted two-cylinder engine driving a four forward and single reverse gearbox. The driving seat was also mounted at the rear, just in front of the engine, leaving plenty of room between the front and rear axles for the mid-mounting of implements such as mowers, hoes and cultivators, these being specially designed items built by David Brown. The little tractor even included an implement lift system worked by compressed air and used the hollow front frame as an air reservoir. Equipped with a four-speed transmission, the 2D was ideal for row crop work on small acreages but it proved to have a pretty limited appeal, despite a narrow vineyard and even an industrial version being produced.

Biggest in the new range was the very impressive 50D. Powered by a six-cylinder engine of 50 hp, this was a very large tractor for its day.

The 50D was large enough to retain the double seat that was last seen on the Cropmaster, and it was also fitted with engine side panels and front headlights mounted on stalks beside the radiator grille.

With its large size the 50D was often used by contractors rather than farmers, and this example has been fitted with a front guard and rear winch as well as an impressive cab.

The 50D was based on the Trackmaster 50 crawler, which later became the 50TD, and used the same six-cylinder diesel power plant.

A rear view of the little David Brown 2D showing the little 14 hp air-cooled diesel engine and wheel mark eradicators.

The 2D incorporated an implement lift system using compressed air held in the hollow frame of the tractor and was ideal for row-crop work, especially for market gardens and similar operations. Using implements in a mid-mounted position gave the driver a superb view of the work at hand.

CHAPTER 2

A New Paradigm

As good as the David Brown tractor range was, it was looking rather outdated by the mid-1950s and so, at the Royal Smithfield Show of 1956, the first in a completely new range of tractors appeared. It was announced among a great deal of fanfare but in the end would prove to be something of a damp squib! However, it still heralded the beginning of a new era for the David Brown tractor.

Called the 900, the new tractor looked larger and more imposing than the 30C and 30D it was designed to replace thanks to a completely new bonnet design. The Hunting Pink colour remained but blue wheel centres and a new radiator grille, also painted blue, joined it. The new front bonnet design also carried the David Brown name centrally in a vertical position between the two sets of grilles. One feature that did remain unaltered from the earlier David Brown machines was the offsetting of the steering column slightly to the right, a feature of David Brown tractors since the VAK1.

There was still a choice of fuels as well with the vaporising oil version putting out 37 hp, the petrol engine 45 hp and the diesel, which was becoming an ever popular option, 40 hp. A six forward and two reverse transmission was fitted and from 1957 a two-speed PTO and TCU hydraulics were added to the mix and at the same time the steering column was centralised. The David Brown badge was also moved from its vertical position on the front grille to a new horizontal position above the grilles themselves at the very top of the bonnet front.

Despite a few high-clearance tricycle-type 900 tractors being built predominantly for the North American export market, the 900 was not a successful tractor. There were many problems with the new fuel injection pump, which reflected poorly on the rest of the tractor and its reliability, despite this not being David Brown's fault and the cause finally being traced back to its suppliers, CAV.

The damage to the 900's credibility had been done though, and so it was decided to replace it with a new model in 1958 – a model that was called the 950. The new tractor was essentially the same as the 900 but, crucially, the new model number and the use of yellow for the wheel centres and radiator grille made it look different to the much-maligned 900 and a new fuel injection system also gave an extra 2.5 hp to the engine output. Tweaks to the steering linkage and drawbar arrangement were also made at the same time.

The David Brown 900 of 1956 saw a radical departure from the rounded bonnet lines of the earlier machines.

The 900 came with a choice of either diesel, petrol, or vaporising oil as a fuel, but the most popular was now the diesel version, which produced 40 hp. The blue front grille and wheel centres really made the 900 stand out as a new breed of tractor from Yorkshire.

Unfortunately the 900 was not a success, with teething troubles being quite severe for a time, mostly attributed to the new fuel injection equipment. It therefore became the tractor that David Brown would rather forget!

The basic design of the 900 was retained when its replacement arrived in 1958, although the new 950 looked quite different with its yellow front grille and wheel centres as well as the new decals. It was also the first of the Implematic tractors.

Above: The David Brown badge showing the Lancashire and Yorkshire roses and the DB initials was fitted to the front above the radiator grille.

Right: Seen on a farm in Somerset, the 950 used a new fuel injection system and was certainly a successful machine, making up well for the shortcomings of the 900.

In 1959 the 950 Implematic arrived with the TCU system, being joined by the Implematic Traction Depth Control system, which, like the Ferguson System, did not require a depth wheel to be fitted to a mounted implement for depth control. This improved the versatility of the new tractor immensely and a David Brown tractor could finally enjoy the full benefits of a Ferguson-type system, with top-link sensing and therefore perfect control of implement depth at all times.

The 950 Implematic was the first of a whole Implematic family of tractors with the next one making its appearance in 1960. The 850 Implematic was a smaller machine, designed to replace the earlier 25 range of models, which had soldiered on next to the 900 and then the 950. It was a 35 hp tractor with the six forward and two reverse transmission, plus Live-Drive PTO and a hydraulic system. A petrol version was also produced for a period.

The 880 and 990 Implematic tractors arrived in 1961 with the 880 being a 42.5 hp tractor while the 990 was a 52 hp machine, which even had the option of an automatic gearbox, meaning that the tractor could sense the optimal gear for whatever task the machine was doing. However, the extra cost put most farmers off buying this advanced system.

Interestingly, an important export deal saw the 850 and 950 painted in the green and white colour scheme of the Oliver Corporation, being sold in the USA as the Oliver 500 and 600 during the early 1960s.

1963 saw an improved 990 model with the option of a twelve-speed gearbox. As the largest and most powerful David Brown tractor yet, the 990 also proved to be one of the most popular as well. Still with 52 hp from its four-cylinder David Brown engine, it also featured an air cleaner tucked away behind the radiator grille.

A 35 hp engine powered the 850, which replaced the 25 models in 1960.

This 850 is still used for topping pastures in East Sussex and, although the paint has faded, it is still in good working order.

The 880 with 42.5 hp arrived in 1961. This is a narrow example for vineyard use.

The 990 was also launched in 1961 and had 52 horses under the bonnet. It was even offered with an automatic gearbox for a short while.

This 990 is in very original unrestored condition, but like a great many David Brown tractors it is still capable of a day's work many decades after it was built.

David Brown engines were extremely well made units and were built to last. The 990 still shared the basic lines of the 900 model.

This 990, complete with David Brown front loader, was used on a farm in East Sussex. Note the fitting of a safety frame, which would have been added following the introduction of legislation in 1970. [Photo: Kim Parks]

Another original 990 seen at a rally in Norfolk. Many of these tractors have survived into preservation, partly because they have had such long working lives beforehand.

Two superbly restored 850 tractors at a show, proving just how effective the new colour scheme was when they would have been new.

A 990 and David Brown front loader that is part of a collection in Somerset.

The new decals on the bonnet sides of the Implematic tractors looked superb, the yellow being picked out well against the black background.

The driving position of the 990 had changed somewhat from the days of the Cropmaster, with a centrally mounted steering wheel and column now the norm, while there are a few more gauges and a hand throttle under the steering wheel itself to the left.

In 1964 the little 770 arrived and would spell the beginning of yet another new era in David Brown tractor design. The 880 also got a new engine in that year when its four-cylinder unit was replaced by a three-cylinder David Brown engine, effectively replacing both the 880 and 950 models.

The word 'Implematic' was conspicuous by its absence on the new three-cylinder, 33 hp 770, which had the word 'Selectamatic' written on the bonnet instead. This new system used a single dial to choose between TCU, depth control, height control or the external hydraulic services, hence the Selectamatic name. This made it much easier to work the tractor at its best whatever the conditions or task it was doing.

The 770 was the last of one era and the first of another as later in 1965 a whole new range of David Brown tractors would appear, all with Selectamatic and all with a new look.

The last ever David Brown tractor to be introduced in the Hunting Pink and yellow livery was the 770. This little 33 hp tractor was also the first Selectamatic model with improved hydraulic system

CHAPTER 3

White Takes Over

The autumn of 1965 saw a whole new image for the David Brown tractor range, as Selectamatic was rolled out across the various different models. After the UK market leaders Ford and Massey Ferguson had unveiled new model ranges in 1964, it was felt that David Brown needed a fresh appearance to compete and so a Chocolate Brown engine and transmission colour was chosen along with Orchid White for the new design of tinwork and Poppy Red for the exhaust stack. All in all the new colour scheme certainly worked as the appearance of the tractors was changed greatly and the new Selectamatic 770, 880 and 990 models were popular machines for the rest of the 1960s. In 1965 the 770 got more power, making it a 36 hp machine, while the 880 became a 46 hp machine and the 990 was also uprated to 55 hp.

With Selectamatic being a standard feature, the David Brown range was now well positioned to take on the competition and, with a range of three models to choose from, there was something for most farmers' requirements. This was further enhanced by the fact that a differential lock, a two-speed power take-off and a six forward by two reverse transmission were all standard equipment and the options list included the twelve by four gearbox at extra cost.

The 770 and 880 both used a David Brown three-cylinder engine, the 770 having a 2.4 litre version, the 880 a slightly larger 2.7 litre unit and the 990 a 3.2 litre four pot motor, also built by David Brown. These power plants were always being praised as reliable and gutsy performers. Indeed, the engines were always a strong selling point of the David Brown tractor.

It took until 1967 before a new model appeared but when it did the new 1200 Selectamatic proved worth the wait. With a four-cylinder engine producing 67 hp, this was the largest David Brown tractor so far and it could be equipped with a six or twelve-speed transmission along with other features such as drum brakes, live hydraulics, independent PTO, power steering and a differential lock.

With a longer bonnet and larger tyres the 1200 was an imposing machine in the late 1960s and its size made it seem much bigger than its 67 hp output might suggest, its four-cylinder David Brown engine having a capacity of 3.6 litres.

From 1965 a new Orchid White and Chocolate Brown livery was adopted. This 770 shows off the new colours and also the slightly revised bonnet design, including the new radiator grilles.

The 770 was still powered by the David Brown three-cylinder engine but tweaks led to it being slightly more powerful with a rating now of 36 hp. Note the '12 Speed' decal next to the model number, denoting the fact that the optional twelve forward and four reverse gearbox is fitted.

With the arrival of the Selectamatic range the 880 became a 46 hp tractor. This one is fitted with the remains of a Lambourn weather cab.

This later 880 is shown at auction, fitted with a Duncan cab that was probably retrofitted sometime in the 1970s.

The new 990 boasted 55 hp and this example has had the front headlights moved up from their usual position half way up the front grille to a higher elevation to allow the fitting of a front loader.

Equipped with David Brown loader and a Lambourn weather cab, this 990 is shown in East Sussex wrapping silage bales. [Photo: Kim Parks]

The 1200 took power up to 67 hp when launched in 1967. Although a four-cylinder engine provided the power, the long bonnet made this tractor look much bigger than the 990.

As the flagship model of the David Brown tractor range, the 1200 certainly looked impressive.

1967 saw a change made to the engine fitted in the 990 model when a similar version to that used in the 1200, but with a shorter stroke, was used instead of the original unit. A new model also appeared in that year, with the 780 making its appearance with 46 hp from its three-cylinder 2.7 litre engine and fitted with Live Drive, plus the option of either six or twelve-speed transmissions.

The 1200 was improved in 1968 when its output was increased to 72 hp and a four-wheel-drive option arrived in 1970 thanks to the factory fitting of an Italian-built Selene front axle, which at the same time was also offered as an option on the 990.

Production of the 1200 continued up to 1971 so it came under the new safety cab legislation that was introduced in the UK during 1970, which required a cab to be fitted to all new tractors that would protect the driver if the tractor overturned. David Brown turned to Sta-Dri for their cabs and this saw the 1200 appear with a rather boxy design, which also required the round rear mudguards fitted previously to be replaced with flat versions. Although it looked pretty rough and ready, it was actually quite a spacious cab by the standards of the day and was certainly an improvement on the earlier after-market weather cabs.

The 780 replaced the 770 in 1967, with the three-cylinder 46 hp engine providing the grunt. This one is ploughing at a working day in Lincolnshire.

A front view of a 780, showing the distinctive lines of the Selectamatic tractors.

The David Brown badge was still placed prominently on the front radiator grille, but now with a white background.

An 880 Selectamatic taking place in a ploughing match in the south of England. This later model would have been fitted with front headlights mounted within the top moulding, although this tractor has lost these along the way as well as the radiator grille itself. [Photo: Kim Parks]

A fully restored Lambourn weather cab complete with cladding and glass adorns this 780 tractor shown in Somerset.

The well-positioned controls of the 780 with the tops of the two centrally mounted gear levers just visible at the bottom.

This poor 990 has seen better days and appears to have been in this same position in a Sussex wood for quite some time, judging by how it has sunk while still being used to power a wood saw.

David Brown had always been a large producer of industrial tractors and this unrestored example is seen at a show complete with Sta-Dri cab.

The Sta-Dri cab was the first type of safety cab to be fitted to David Brown tractors following the 1970 cab legislation and was used until the firm's own cab was ready.

David Brown were ahead of the competition by offering factory-fitted four-wheel drive on the 990 and 1200 from 1970. A Selene front axle was used, as shown on this 990 taking part in a ploughing match. [Photo: Kim Parks]

A four-wheel drive 1200 at a show. This model had been uprated to 72 hp in 1968. [Photo: Kim Parks]

Four-wheel drive improved the pulling ability of the 1200 substantially.

This equal-size wheel, four-wheel drive conversion of the 1200 must have had superb pulling power.

CHAPTER 4

The Power Game

Other new models followed thick and fast during the early 1970s, all with the Selectamatic hydraulic system. The smallest model in the range was now the new 885, powered by a three-cylinder 2.7 litre engine of 48 hp and fitted with twelve-speed synchromesh transmission. Replacing the 780 and the 880, the new 885, with its slight increase in power, became a very popular model, as it was ideal for small farms or as a general runabout on larger arable estates. It was also very frugal on fuel use and also pretty light for its size.

Next up was a new four-cylinder 990 model, now a 58 hp machine, while the new 995 and 996 tractors were identical with the same power rating of 64 hp from their four-cylinder motors, but the 996 differed by having a separate hand clutch for the live PTO. Both the 995 and 996 shared the four-cylinder 3.6 litre David Brown engine.

The 1210 and 1212 replaced the 1200 and were powered by the same four-cylinder 3.6 litre 72 hp motor. The 1212 was identical to the 1210 except for the fact that it was fitted with a new revolutionary gearbox called Hydrashift. This was a semi-automatic transmission that had twelve forward and four reverse gears that could be selected on the move by four clutchless gears in each of the three forward ratios and one in reverse, making this one of the first semi-powershift transmissions offered on a British tractor. As befitting a company still heavily involved in gear manufacture, David Brown now had one of the most advanced tractor transmissions on the market. A small lever mounted up on the new-look dashboard was used for the clutchless changes and the system went on to win several design awards.

In 1970 new safety cab legislation in the UK led to tractor manufacturers having to supply new machines with a cab that would protect the driver in the event of a roll-over accident. This meant that the cab's frame had to be strong enough to take the full weight of the tractor it was mounted on without any major deformation. As we mentioned earlier, David Brown used Sta-Dri cabs up to now but designed their own unique cab to meet the legislation, the resultant cab being a very tall affair with an open rear initially, and very small doors. Although it met all the necessary requirements, the David Brown cab was probably not the best, and despite large glass windows it always felt as though you were sitting rather low when operating the tractor when this cab was fitted.

The new 995 was a 64 hp tractor, had new bonnet decals with a bold red background, and this one is fitted with the new David Brown safety cab.

The cab designed by David Brown was unique. It was very tall, angular, and included extremely narrow doors – but it worked!

Seen at a Cheffins auction in
Cambridgeshire, this 1210 shows off
the new decals and the safety cab.
It replaced the 1200 model.

The new 885 was the smallest tractor in the range with the deletion of the 780. This tractor,
used daily on a Sussex livestock farm, shows the short-lived new-style decals, including the
'bottle-opener' David Brown logo.

A three-cylinder 48 hp David Brown diesel engine resided under the bonnet of the 885. For a yardscraper tractor, this 885 is still remarkably sound, although the rust is beginning to take hold of the bonnet and the left-hand side headlamp has received a battering!

It was all to change in 1972, however, when American oil giant Tenneco acquired the David Brown Tractor division from the parent company and merged it with its own North American J. I. Case operation.

The J. I. Case firm had its origins back in 1842 at Racine in Wisconsin when Jerome Increase Case founded the J. I. Case Threshing Machine Co. The first successful smaller Case tractors arrived as early as 1915 in the form of some rather unusual looking Crossmount machines with a transverse mounted engine. These were later followed by more conventional Model C and L tractors in the 1930s before the arrival of the more refined Model R and D at the end of the decade, with the DEX export version built from 1941 being popular in the UK.

During the 1950s Case tractors grew in size and sophistication but were not now offered in Europe, at least not until the takeover of David Brown in 1972. From the following year the big six-cylinder Case 970 Agri-King with its 101 hp engine was offered on the UK market, as a flagship model above and beyond the largest tractor built at Meltham at that time, the 72 hp 1212 and 1210.

Despite the changes, tractor production at Meltham carried on as before. Although a new livery saw the white tinwork remain, the chocolate mechanicals were replaced by red, including the wheel centres, making the tractors look even more imposing – especially when brand new and shiny!

J. I. Case has a very long history in agricultural machinery and produced its first tractor in 1915. The Crossmotor tractors had an unusual engine layout but were very successful and laid a firm foundation for later tractor models.

The Case Model C of the 1930s was a very capable machine and used a more familiar engine layout.

A superbly restored example of the Case DEX tractor, designed for export to the UK in particular. These would be among the last sold in Britain until 1972.

With a change to white livery, the Agri King range of Case high-horsepower, two-wheel-drive tractors were all six-cylinder powerhouses, this 1370 being a good example of the breed.

With the takeover by J. I. Case under Tenneco ownership, the Case name appeared on the bonnet sides, although fairly small, and the wheel centres and engine became red. Note the fuel tank mounted on top of the bonnet just in front of the cab on this 885, shown ready for work with a harrow in East Sussex.

This Suffolk-based 885 is equipped with a Quicke front loader and the David Brown quiet cab derived from the earlier safety cab and fitted from 1976.

A narrow version of the 885 seen taking a break from mowing. It is fitted with a very extensive safety frame, which no doubt also protected the operator from branches in its previous life on a vineyard or orchard.

The driver's platform of the narrow 885, showing the hand throttle still mounted to the right of the steering wheel on the dashboard and the two gear levers mounted over the transmission tunnel.

The 885 shows the new bonnet decals introduced after the merger in 1972. These were much neater than before and looked good with the white on black. David Brown engines were still used exclusively across the range.

Another 885 with the same safety frame, this time being used to power a saw bench in Sussex.

This industrial version of the 885 was used in its former life by the Greater London Council and is fitted with a David Brown front loader. It now fulfils a much smaller role on a farm in East Sussex.

A view into the cab, showing how the David Brown safety cab was pretty cramped, although the large front windscreen did allow good forward visibility.

This immaculate 990 looks like new but is still pretty much in original condition and used regularly on a small farm in Suffolk. It is fitted with the David Brown-designed and built quiet cab.

By contrast, this 995 in East Sussex is equipped with the earlier safety cab. It has a concrete weight mounted to the rear linkage to counterbalance the silage bale on the front of the David Brown loader. [Photo: Kim Parks]

The 996 was identical to the 995, except for the addition of a hand clutch for its live PTO. Once again this is a Sussex example complete with David Brown front loader and rear concrete weight.

The 996 clearly shows the David Brown quiet cab fitted from 1976. Removal of the door allows easier and quicker access to and from the cab, which is handy because the gap is not exactly spacious!

The 1210 replaced the 1200 and this Suffolk example is fitted with the quiet cab. Its long bonnet belies its relatively modest 72 hp.

Inside the David Brown quiet cab, showing the improved instrument cluster and new position of the hand throttle to the left-hand side of the dashboard. It was still very much a cramped environment in which to spend a working day.

The back end of the 1210, showing the link arms and the clevis hitch drawbar.

The 1410 was a large and sophisticated tractor in its day with its 91 hp turbocharged engine and Hydrashift transmission. Fitted with David Brown's own quiet cab, this very tidy example lives in Lincolnshire.

The 1212 was the same as the 1210 except for the inclusion of the revolutionary new Hydrashift transmission, which gave clutchless changes through three ratios on the move.

In 1975 the David Brown Case 1410 with synchromesh transmission and the 1412 with Hydrashift were launched. Both were powered by the same four-cylinder, 3.6 litre, 91 hp engine. A first, though, was the fact that the engine used in these models was the first from David Brown to feature a turbocharger. Most tractor manufacturers had been a bit cautious when it came to using this relatively new engine technology and, although high horsepower tractors in the USA had been using turbochargers from the late 1960s, it took until 1971 and the success of the 94 hp Ford 7000 before it was really accepted in the UK.

The engine on the 1410 and 1412 was beefed up to cope with turbocharging and also included a dry air cleaner for maximum protection from dust and dirt. In 1976 a four-wheel drive version of the 1410 was introduced, the synchromesh transmission allowing this while the Hydrashift could not be adapted to take four-wheel drive at this time. The front drive axles were now sourced from Kramer.

It was in 1976 that new quiet cab legislation came into force in Britain, brought about by the very noisy environment of the earlier safety cabs. David Brown modified its own safety cab design to meet the requirements, but this cab was still not very easy to access thanks to the small doorframes. The extra cladding needed, plus the enclosed rear, made them rather claustrophobic to boot! One advantage over the older safety cab version was the higher driving position that was introduced, but compared to the competition, the David Brown offering still seemed rather lacking in many respects, even if it was very distinctive!

In 1977 a special tractor with silver cab and a purple roof was exhibited and sold by auction at the Royal Smithfield Show with the proceeds going to the Queen's Jubilee Appeal. The model chosen was a 1412 with the David Brown quiet cab and it caused quite a stir at the show that year.

This well-used 1210 is at the Cheffins auction near Ely and shows the better-appointed Sekura quiet cab, which replaced the David Brown version.

This 1212 is also fitted with the Sekura Q cab, as well as narrow row crop wheels on the rear.

Sands Agricultural Machinery, based in Norfolk, used many David Brown skid units for their range of self-propelled sprayers. Making use of a David Brown engine and gearbox, this SAM sprayer is seen working in oilseed rape in Suffolk.

A better alternative to the David Brown-built quiet cab arrived when the firm started fitting cabs built by Sekura, of a similar design to that fitted to John Deere and International Harvester tractors of the time, and later also to Ford tractors. The operator now had a much better environment in which to spend a working day and it put the final touches to what was an excellent range of tractors, the cab being perhaps the only major let-down prior to the arrival of the Sekura unit.

CHAPTER 5

Tractors for the Eighties

The Case name had been used on the sides of tractor bonnets for some time when the new 90 Series were launched in 1979, but the David Brown name was always still the most prominent. This remained the case on the new 90 Series range, replacing all the previous David Brown tractor models and also including new six-cylinder Case machines built at Racine, which had first been seen in the United States in 1977.

The five new David Brown models all looked very different to any tractors built at Meltham previously, although underneath the new tinwork many of the models were very similar mechanically to what had gone before. The new slightly sloping bonnets with headlights included in the front radiator surround gave cleaner lines than previously and the new Explorer cab supplied by Sekura topped all this off. With wide-opening doors and a comfortable suspended seat, flat floor, large glass area and modern fitments, this was definitely the best cab so far fitted to a David Brown tractor! Basically the same cab would also be used on Leyland and later Marshall tractors, but the internal fitments would remain unique to each manufacturer.

The 90 Series range certainly looked the part in 1979, with the 1190 being the smallest at 48 hp and the only one to use a three-cylinder engine, of 2.7 litres. As the base model the 1190 was only offered with the standard twelve forward by four reverse synchromesh transmission, and was only built in two-wheel-drive form. The 58 hp 3.2 litre 1290 shared the same specification, as did the 67 hp 3.6 litre 1390, but both had the option of a four-wheel drive version. The 1490, at 83 hp, was the largest four-cylinder tractor in the range, with a 3.6 litre engine, while the top spot was taken by the 5.4 litre, 103 hp, six-cylinder 1690. Both of the largest tractors were offered in either two or four-wheel-drive configurations.

Five of the big six-cylinder Case tractors built at Racine in the States were also offered in the UK as part of the 90 Series, giving power outputs from 120 to 273 hp. In 1981 the big six-cylinder range, built in the USA and offered in the UK, had increased with the addition of the monster 4690 and 4890 with twelve-speed powershift transmission and advanced four-wheel steering system.

1982 saw several upgrades to the 90 Series, including a new type of bonnet that hinged at the front to give much better access to the engine compartment and with higher front headlights, raised from the bottom of the radiator grille to a new position above it. Up to now, David Brown had fitted its own design of a four-wheel drive front axle to the 90 Series but from 1982 these were sourced from Carraro in Italy.

The 1390 was a 67 hp tractor and this example seen mowing in Suffolk is a fairly early model and shows the lines of the new 90 Series David Brown tractors very well.

The bonnet of the 1390 showing the new lines of the 90 Series bonnet with the front headlights mounted below the front radiator grille and the fitting of the Case badge on the front.

Fitted with the new Explorer cab built by Sekura and fitted out by David Brown, the 1390 looks very modern for a machine launched in 1979. It was also adopted by fellow British manufacture Leyland for their new models introduced in 1980.

The 90 Series was also offered in a high clearance version, as shown here by this example at the Cheffins auction.

The 1190 was the smallest model of the 90 Series with a 48 hp three-cylinder motor. This is an example of the later 90 Series models following the revision of the bonnet, including higher set headlights above the front grille. [Photo: Kim Parks]

The 1290 was a 58 hp tractor and this example works on a farm in East Sussex.

The new design of bonnet gave better access and this close-up of the 1290 clearly shows the power steering ram beside the engine fitted to the front axle.

David Brown engines were used throughout the new 90 Series range.

The Case badge was now mounted to the bottom right of the front radiator grille and, with the Sekura cab and clean bonnet lines, the 90 Series was certainly an impressive-looking machine.

This side view also shows the fuel tank mounted under the cab behind the steps.

At 83 hp the 1490 was a useful size of tractor and this very clean example lives in the Republic of Ireland.

A rear view of the 1290 shows the business end of the tractor, with wide mudguards and the David Brown name written on the back of the cab roof.

David Brown loaders were still available for the 90 Series and were also still very popular with many users. This 1490 is picking up hay bales in East Sussex. [Photo: Kim Parks]

Largest of the 90 Series, and the most powerful David Brown tractor yet produced, was the 1690, at 105 hp in Mark II guise. Available in both two- and four-wheel-drive forms, this two-wheel-drive example at a Cheffins auction certainly looks a big machine.

With the 90 Series already existing in North America for a year or two before the David Brown tractors made their debut, the final range stretched from the little 1190 to the massive four-wheel-drive, four-wheel-steer North American giants such as the 4690.

It was also in 1982 that the 1690 gained a couple of more horses thanks to a Holset turbocharger being fitted to produce 105 hp and several other mechanical improvements were also made.

The 1390 also got the benefit of the Hydrashift option the following year and the 1690 also saw several improvements late in its life to resolve some reliability issues.

CHAPTER 6

Last of the Line

1983 proved to be a landmark year. After eleven years of David Brown Tractors being part of J. I. Case, the David Brown name was finally dropped in favour of simply Case with the introduction of the new 94 Series tractors.

Essentially improved versions of the earlier 90 Series, the 94 Series were painted in a new livery – still white for the tinwork but with black replacing the former Power Red engine and transmission. This was done, according to some, to hide all the oil leaks that were clearly visible on the earlier 90 Series tractors!

The range appeared on the surface to be direct developments of the original 90 Series, with the numbering system carrying on as before, but underneath the engines had been greatly altered. Most unchanged was the 1194, which replaced the 1190 and remained as the only three-cylinder model in the range at 48 hp, as well as being the only one not to be offered with the option of four-wheel drive.

The 1294 now had three extra horses at 61 hp from its four-cylinder block while the 1394 had an extra 5 hp thanks to a turbocharger boosting output to 72 hp.

The 1494 was also turbocharged but retained the same 83 hp rating as the earlier 1490 model. The 1594, however, was a completely new model with 95 hp available from a 5.4 litre six-cylinder engine. The 1694 was the biggest of the 94 Series built in the UK and had a turbocharged six-cylinder engine of 108 hp.

A creeper box was available for the 1394 and 1494 models and with the possibility now of four-wheel-drive Hydroshift transmissions, the 1694 was only now offered with this and four-wheel-drive. A tradition of offering high clearance models saw the 1294, 1394 and 1494 being offered in this form and also the production of a conversion kit.

With its distinctive new look the 94 Series not only sorted out the teething troubles of the original 90 Series, it did much more, bringing to the marketplace a thoroughly modern and up to date tractor range with generous specification and, tied as it was into the larger six-cylinder American Case range, offered a full line-up of different models to suit all farming requirements.

The 94 Series had only been in production for a couple of years when Tenneco bought the International Harvester business and merged it with Case to form Case IH.

This baby of the new 94 Series, the 1194, shows clearly the new look of this 1983 range and the lack of a David Brown badge.

The 1294 not only received the new look, it also got extra horses, making it a 61 hp machine.

This four-wheel drive 1294 shows off the new Case branding very clearly.

Based in East Sussex, this 1294 is now just used for light duties around a farm that has been converted into stabling for horses.

The 1394 now featured a turbocharged engine producing 72 hp – more than enough for this example to collect grass for silage with a Krone self-loading forage wagon in East Sussex.

The condition of this 1394 certainly hides the fact that it has been a main prime-mover on this farm for many years.

The brackets for a front loader can be seen attached to this 1394 when seen from the side. By 1983, when the 94 Series appeared, the Sekura Explorer cab was also being used by Marshall Tractors after taking over the British Leyland tractor range.

The 1594 was a new six-cylinder model with 95 hp available, shown here with a Case loader on an East Sussex farm.

This 1594 at auction clearly shows the Hydra-Shift badge now positioned under the Case name on both sides of the bonnet. Extra work lights have been fitted to the front of the cab roof for extended after-dark working.

The 1694 was the largest British-built Case tractor with its six-cylinder engine featuring a turbocharger and producing 108 hp. This fine machine, dirty from spreading fertilizer in sticky conditions, is the largest tractor on a farm in the south-east of England.

Baling silage with a Case 1694 and Krone KR120 round baler. Hydra-Shift was now also available on four-wheel-drive tractors after being exclusively offered on only two-wheel-drive machines previously. [Photo: Kim Parks]

View from the driving seat of a Case 1694, showing the much more sophisticated dashboard layout of these machines, plus the hand throttle to the right of the binnacle.

With a comprehensive range of models being produced in the IH factory in Doncaster, as well as factories in the USA and in Europe, it was inevitable that the ex-David Brown product would suffer at some point and, in the end, both the 1194 and 1294 models would be discontinued.

From 1985 both the IH and Case tractor ranges were produced in a new red and black livery with black wheel centres and grey rims. Despite the reduction in the number of tractor models built in Yorkshire, the now Case IH-branded 94 Series was still proving relatively popular and looked particularly smart in the new corporate livery.

It was obvious that in a time of reduced farm incomes, and therefore fewer farmers spending money on new tractors, further rationalisation would be inevitable and it was decided that out of the Doncaster and Huddersfield factories, it would be Doncaster that would be kept on as the 1980s drew to a close.

The 94 Series soldiered on until 1988 when the Meltham Mills factory was finally closed, the last tractors built that year all featuring special Commemorative Edition decals on the bonnet sides along with the old David Brown logo and the words: 'Over 50 Years of Service 1936–1988'. It was the end of an era and the world would never see the likes of such a tractor firm again.

Two well-kept examples of the Case IH 1394 that was first seen in 1985 following the merger of Case and International Harvester. Tractors built in Meltham had returned to red paint after twenty years of being white!

Based on a small farm in Suffolk, this 1394 Hydra-Shift is seen dropping off a trailer of bales in a partly completed barn.

The new red colour combined with black looked very good on the new 94 Series bonnets. It took a while before the now more familiar Case IH name was adopted on the tractors, the Case International name being used for some time.

A rear view of the Case IH 1394 clearly shows the clean lines of these tractors and the new black wheel centres with grey rims.

Hydra-Shift earned its place on the sides of tractor bonnets equipped with it. It was one of the very first successful semi-powershift transmissions and perhaps deserves more recognition than it does today.

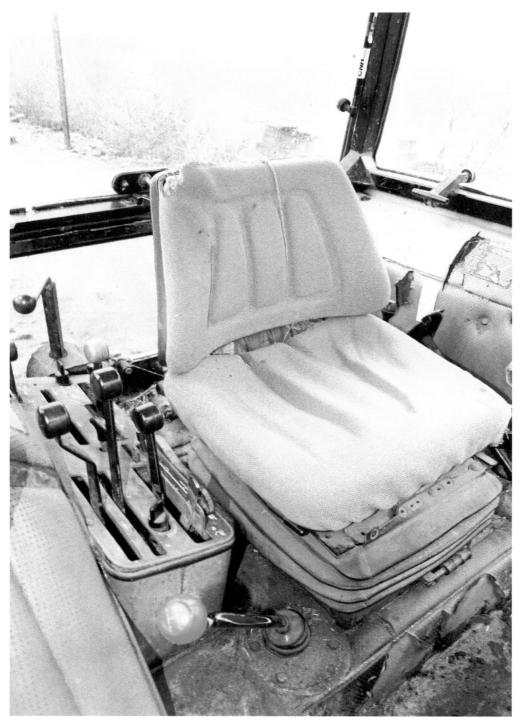

A comfortable suspended seat awaited the operator of the 1394, with all the main controls mounted to the right of it. Note how the main gear lever is now mounted to the side, leaving space for an uncluttered flat floor in the cab.

The hydraulic, PTO and four-wheel drive controls to the right of the driving seat in the 1394.

The clear and concise dashboard was carried over from the earlier 94 Series.

High-clearance models were still available such as this 1394 with front and back sprayer, making it a suitable alternative to a self-propelled unit. [Photo: Kim Parks]

A two-wheel-drive 1594 at Cheffins emphasises the long, sleek bonnet that conceals the six-cylinder engine.

A four-wheel drive 1594 at the Cheffins auction awaiting a new owner.

During the last year of tractor production at Meltham, in 1988, special Commemorative Edition decals were fitted to the bonnets of tractors, which also included a special reappearance of the David Brown badge.

A 1394 Commemorative Edition at Cheffins. As the last David Brown tractors to be built, these machines are pretty collectable today.

CHAPTER 7

David Brown Legacy

Although the David Brown tractor factory was no more after 1988, the main part of the company continues to produce gears in Huddersfield and the tractor legacy also lives on.

Case IH tractors continued with both Case and IH 'DNA' and designs, but the engineers at Meltham had also been working on what would have been a successor to the 94 Series, with even some prototype 96 Series tractors having been built. At the heart of the new models was a new four-stage semi-powershift transmission evolved from Hydrashift, plus a re-worked Sekura Explorer cab. These designs eventually saw the light of day, mated to new engines built in a joint venture between Case IH and Cummins, as the Maxxum 5100 Series. Although built in the former IH factory at Neuss in Germany, the Maxxum owed a lot of its design elements to the David Brown 94 and 90 Series.

The Maxxum range was launched in 1990 and was only the second new range of tractors since the formation of Case IH back in 1985; the high-horsepower Magnum range, based heavily on American IH designs, was the first in 1988. Three models made up the Maxxum range when they first appeared, starting with the four-cylinder 90 hp 5120, then the 100 hp six-cylinder 5130 and finally the six-cylinder 110 hp 5140. The Hydrashift transmission had evolved into a sixteen forward and twelve reverse semi-powershift that also incorporated a clutchless forward and reverse shuttle, making the Maxxum range the most advanced at that time in its power class. For those purchasers who did not want such a high level of sophistication, all the models were also available with a Synchro gearbox in place of the semi-powershift.

Although on first glance the Maxxum might not have seemed to have much to do with David Brown, on closer inspection the bonnet lines certainly looked similar to the 94 Series, with headlights mounted in the front grille in the same style. The cab looked very modern with its large roof moulding and wide rear mudguards but again, looking closer, the Sekura Explorer cab frame is clearly evident. Inside the cab however, it was a very different story and there was not much that a David Brown driver of old would find familiar. All the main controls, including the gear levers, were mounted up on a pedestal to the right of the driving seat and a digital dashboard provided information on tractor performance. The engines, however, were certainly very different, being Cummins units developed in a new venture with Case IH, known as CDC, and brought in a new generation of power and performance A new flagship model arrived later when the 125 hp 5150 joined the range, still using the CDC engine but breaking the 120 hp barrier.

In 1995 the second-generation Maxxum tractors arrived with the Plus models. New-style decals and the word 'Plus' on the bottom of the front radiator grille denoted the new range, which also included a neutral position on the forward and reverse shuttle.

The final incarnation of the German Maxxum range was the Pro Series, which included a taller cab to provide more headroom for the driver and a new layout for the gear controls, the sliding powershift control lever having now been replaced by a new thumb switch for engaging the four powershift ratios. A colourful 'Pro' decal on the bonnet sides made it easy to tell the new tractors apart from their predecessors.

Thus, the David Brown legacy continued up until 1997, when a completely new range of Maxxum MX models began production at Doncaster in Yorkshire. These bore little in common with the David Brown tractors of a decade before and so it was, finally, the end of an era.

The David Brown factory might have closed in 1988 but the designs from there lived on with the Case IH Maxxum range of 1990. This is the second model in the range, the six-cylinder 100 hp 5130, which could be seen as a modern-day 1594.

The control binnacle to the right of the driver's seat in the Maxxum was very different. At far left can be seen the powershift lever for the four ratios while the main gear lever is just partially visible above it.

The Maxxum 5140 at 110 hp was the largest in the Maxxum range initially and equates roughly to the 108 hp 1694. If you look closely at the Maxxum bonnet and cab, similarities become apparent. This is the later Plus version.

A later addition, the 5150, took the Maxxum into 125 hp, and later 132 hp territory, and remained the largest model of the range until the new MX models began production in Doncaster. Built at the IH factory in Neuss, Germany, the original Maxxum tractors were the last development of the David Brown 90 Series.

Two different generations of David Brown at work together – 885 and 1390.

Of course, the David Brown name still lives on with the great number of tractors still out there working on farms and smallholdings. The simplicity and ruggedness of the David Brown design means that these tractors will be able to be kept on working for many years to come. In the annuals of tractor history the David Brown name has an important place, starting with the development and building of the first Ferguson tractor, which led to the revolutionary Type A, through the production of tractors for the war effort, the popular Cropmaster and then the advanced Implematic and Selectamatic ranges of the 1950s and '60s. The firm was always at the forefront of technology and development, recognising early on the importance of four-wheel drive versions of its models and also, of course, producing the Hydroshift transmission, which was world-beating when introduced and was still pretty advanced when the 94 Series disappeared in 1988. Looking back, was Case IH right to favour the Doncaster factory over the old David Brown Meltham site? Well, yes, probably because the Doncaster plant was much more modern and was already set up for the future, whereas Meltham was always dogged by the problems of using old buildings on a full site. In the end though, even the Doncaster factory fell, being closed in 2002.

David Brown will always remain synonymous with the very best of British tractor manufacturing and that is how it should be. There are also several enthusiasts clubs who keep the name flying, and so it looks as though the David Brown legacy is set to last for a long time to come, and that can surely only be a good thing!

A fine line-up of Selectamatic models at a show in Lincolnshire.

This line-up of 25, 25D and 30D tractors looks superb at a rally and keeps the era of these tractors alive.

The David Brown Club stand at a big tractor show in Newark. Several generations of 'Hunting Pink' tractor are visible here, keeping alive the legacy of the David Brown tractor for future generations to enjoy.